CELEBRATING SIXTY-YEARS OF ARLENE AND ANTON'S FAMILY

Anton Paul Sohn MD

TotalRecall Publications, Inc.
1103 Middlecreek
Friendswood, Texas 77546
281-992-3131 281-482-5390 Fax
www.totalrecallpress.com

All rights reserved. Except as permitted under the United States Copyright Act of 1976, No part of this publication may be reproduced, stored in a retrieval system, or transmitted in any form or by any means electronic or mechanical or by photocopying, recording, or otherwise without prior permission of the publisher. Exclusive worldwide content publication/distribution by TotalRecall Publications, Inc.

Copyright © 2023 by Anton P. Sohn MD
Front cover photo: Kris, Arlene, Eric, APS, and Phil
Copy Editor: Kristin Sohn Fermoile MD
Graphics Copyright © by Anton P. Sohn MD

ISBN: 978-1-64883-265-9
UPC: 6-43977-42659-8

FIRST EDITION   1   2   3   4   5   6   7   8   9   10

Colophon is trademarked

The scanning, uploading and distribution of this book via the Internet or via any other means without the permission of the publisher is illegal and punishable by law. Please purchase only authorized electronic editions, and do not participate in or encourage electronic piracy of copyrighted materials. Your support of the author's rights is appreciated.

THIS BOOK IS DEDICATED TO
OUR CHILDREN
ANTON PHILLIP, ERIC ALLAN,
AND KRISTIN DIANE;
OUR GRANDCHILDREN
ANTON PETER, ALEXANDER WISE
KERRY THOMAS, BRADY CARSON,
SIERRA MORGAN, AND ISABELLA JOLIE

ILLUSTRATIONS AND CONTENTS

Acknowledgements	VI
Introduction.	VII
Abbreviations	VIII
1963, Beginning in Indianapolis, Honeymoon, Badlands, S. Dakota	1
1964, Mt. Rainier, Sun Valley, Ohms Park, Olympic Peninsula	2
1965, Trout Lake Camping, Westport Fishing, and Christmas	3
1966, Anton Phillip Born April 28, APS U.S. Army, and California	4
1967-8, San Francisco, Reno, Nevada, and California	5
1969, Eric Allan Born March 24, Reno, Mom with Grandchildren	6
1970, New Home in Reno, Christmas, and "Food for Thought"	7
1971, Kristin Diane Born March 20, Reno, Pyramid Lk & Christmas	8
1972, Middlefork Float Trip, Virgin Islands, and Bodie, Nevada	9
1973, Denmark, Budapest Gypsy Night, Legoland, and Chicago	10
1974, Tahoe Donner Cabin, Alcatraz, and Canada Train Ride	11
1975, Navajo Nat. Monument, Butch Cassidy House, and Easter	12
1976, Tahoe Donner, Indianapolis, and Brown County, Indiana	13
1977, Death Valley, First School, Day, Christmas, and Camping	14
1978, Alaska, Thanksgiving, Christmas, and San Francisco	15
1979, Indy 500 Exhibit, Blue Lake, Chukar Hunt, Donner Lake	16
1980, Puerto Rico, Napa, Indianapolis, and Bower's Mansion, Nev.	17
1981, Chukar Hunt, Salmon Fishing, Christmas, and Eric birthday	18
1982, Donner Lake House, Deer Feast, and New Sail Boat	19
1983, Hawaii, Halloween, Deer Hunt, and Christmas	20
1984, APS NSMA Pres, and Phil - Mass. Inst. of Technology	21
1985, Chichén Itza, Reno Galaxy Crash, and Mexico	22
1986, Hawaii, Minnesota Canoe Trip, and "Go IU"	23
1987, Eric HS Grad, Kris/Mark HS Prom, Deer Hunt, and Florida	24
1988, Eric to USC, Caribbean Cruise, Howe '53 Class Reunion	25
1989, Phil MIT Grad, Kris/Mark Prom, Suzanne/Greg Sohn Wed	26
1990, Kris - UCSB, PC, DL, Eric USC grad, Liz/Phil Sohn Wedding	27
1991, Kris Semester-at-Sea, Christmas, and Donner Lake	28
1992, Pistol Creek Fishing and Hunting, Baltimore, and Christmas	29
1993, Kristin UCSB Grad, FL, San Francisco, and Channel Islands	30
1994, Anton Peter Born Nov. 29, Woodinville, and Christmas	31

1995, Anton Peter one-year-old, APS Skiing, Kristin/Mark to Utah	32
1996, New Orleans, California, Florida, and Eric Sohn MD	33
1997, Kerry Thomas Born March 10, Alexander Wise Born June 24	34
1997, Yolanda/Craig Sohn Wedding, June 14	34
1998, Arlene/APS' Grandchildren and Arlene with Siblings	35
1999, Ephesus, Donner Lake, and Brady Carson Born June 9	36
2000, Sierra Morgan Born Sept. 27, Christmas, FL, and Legoland	37
2001, Tahiti, Ireland, Cupertino. Indianapolis, and Reno, Nevada	38
2002, Pistol Creek, Woodinville, San Diego, and New Lexus	39
2003, Kristin/Mark Fermoile's Wedding, August 9	40
2004, Pistol Creek, California, and Spokane, Washington	41
2005, Pistol Creek, Florida, and Egypt	42
2006, California, Pistol Creek, Australia, Napa, and Halloween	43
2007, Florida, Scotland, Pistol Creek, Christmas, and Bodie, NV	44
2008, Florida, Alaska, Houston, and Lake Tahoe	45
2009, Eric/Mauriza Wedding, APS Retire, PC, DL, and Oregon	46
2010, Sacramento, Hawaii, PC, DL, Spokane, and Woodinville	47
2011, Isabella Jolie Born Feb. 27, and Florida	48
2012, Kristin MD, USC, Pistol Creek, CA, and Isabella Birthday	49
2013. 50th Wed. Anniv, Peter Eagle Scout, DL, PC & Disney Cruise	50
2014, Oregon, PC, Florida, DL, Peter HS Grad, and Woodinville	51
2015, PC, DL, Spokane, Indpls, Kerry HS Grad, and Sacramento	52
2016, PC, DL, Indpls, Alex HS Grad, Reno, and Woodinville	53
2017, Pistol Creek, Donner Lake, Florida, and Sacramento	54
2018, Pistol Creek, Donner Lake, Christmas, and Reno, Nevada	55
2019, Kerry Navy, Sierra AU, Peter Ariz. U Grad, and APS' 84 BD	56
2020, Spokane, New Orleans, Utah, and Kristin's New BMW	57
2021, Brady ASU Grad, AS/APS 58 Wed. Anniv, Kerry U.S. Navy	58
2022, KY Derby, Camp Lejeune, Donner Lk, Ala U, and Reno	59
2023, Sierra Alabama U. Grad, New Orleans, and Reno, Nevada	60
2023, AS/APS' 60th Wed. Anniv. with Children & Grandchildren	61
Postscript: Sky's-The-Limit	62
Index	64

ACKNOWLEDGEMENTS

Note: the following individuals have supplied information for this edition. A book of this scope with detailed history and data on family history would not have been possible without the help of the following individuals. Unnamed others have supplied photos and important information.

Kristin Sohn Fermoile edited this book and supplied photos and history.

Anton Phillip (Phil) Sohn supplied photos and history.

Eric Allan Sohn supplied photos and history.

Bruce Moran of TotalRecall Press published my earlier books and provided motivation to publish this book.

INTRODUCTION

When I was growing up in Irvington on the eastside of Indianapolis, the Sohn family kept a family album of black and white photographs on a shelf in the dining room. My mother divided the album and gave parts to my sister, Anna Louise, my brother, William, and me. Many of the photos I received are displayed in my book, *The Straight and Narrow: Four Hundred Years of Sohn and Fulton History*.

It is my intent to establish a photo album of family events beginning with Arlene and my marriage in 1963 and extending to 2023, our sixth wedding anniversary. Arlene and I have been blessed with three intelligent children, Anton Phillip, Eric Allan, and Kristin Diane, who have successful careers. We have six beautiful grandchildren, Anton Peter, Alexander Wise, Kerry Thomas, Brady Carson, Sierra Morgan, and Isabella Jolie. Our children and grandchildren are highlighted in this book. I will also feature trips and important events during Arlene and my sixty years of marriage.

ABBREVIATIONS

Alex	Alexander Sohn	Mark F	Mark Fermoile
APS	Anton Paul Sohn	Mark H	Mark Hedegard
AS	Arlene Sohn	Mauriza	Mauriza Sohn
Bill	Bill Sohn	MaryJane	MaryJane Alexander
Bob	Robert F. Sohn	Helen	Helen Hedegard
Chris	Christopher Sohn	Mimi	Mimi Sohn
Craig	Craig Sohn	Mom	Ruth Marie Sohn
Danielle	Danielle Hedegard	NSMA	Nev. St. Med. Assoc.
David	David Walker	PC	Pistol Creek
DL	Donner Lake	Peter	Anton Peter Sohn
Earl	WMC laundry worker	Phil	Anton Phillip Sohn
Einger	Einger Sorensen	Rob	Robt. Anthony Sohn
Eric	Eric Sohn	Ron	Ron Cudek
Harold	Harold Hedegard	Ruth	Ruth Gleason
Harriett	Harriett Sohn	Scott	Scott Cudek
Helen	Helen Hedegard	Sierra	Sierra Sohn
Isabella	Isabella Sohn	Stephanie	Stephanie Hedegard
Jane	Jane Hedegard	Suzanne	Suzanne Sohn Carr
Kris	Kristin Sohn	Sven	Sven Hedegard
Kurt	Kurt Hedegard	TD	Tahoe Donner
Laurrie	Laurrie Walker	TDC	Tahoe Donner cabin
Liz	Elizabeth Sohn	Tyler	Tyler Hedegard
Lorie	Kurt's friend	UCSB	Univ. Cal. S. Barbara
Louise	Louise Sohn Walker	Yolanda	Yolanda Sohn

1963, BEGINNING IN INDIANAPOLIS, HONEYMOON, BADLANDS, S. DAKOTA

JUNE 15, ARLENE AND APS

ARLENE, BADLANDS, SOUTH DAKOTA, HONEYMOON

ARLENE, OCT. 12, TACOMA

1964, LIFE IN TACOMA, WASHINGTON

APS, MT. RAINIER SUMMIT, MARCH 13

ARLENE, SUN VALLEY

ARLENE, OLYMPIA, WASHINGTON

ARLENE, BRIDALVEIL FALLS

ARLENE, MOM, OLYMPIC PENNESULA

ARLENE, OHMS PARK, WENANATCHEE

1965, LIFE IN TACOMA, WASHINGTON

APS, UPPER GREEN LAKE, WASHINGTON

ARLENE, TROUT LAKE, WASHINGTON

ARLENE, WESTPORT, WASHINGTON

APS, ARLENE, CHRISTMAS

1966, ANTON PHILLIP BORN APRIL 28

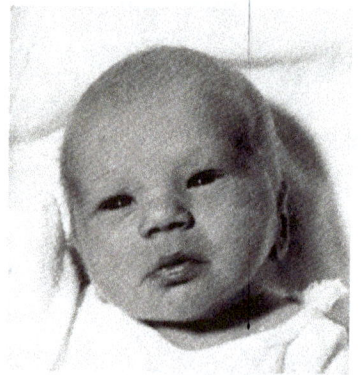

PHIL APRIL 28, TACOMA

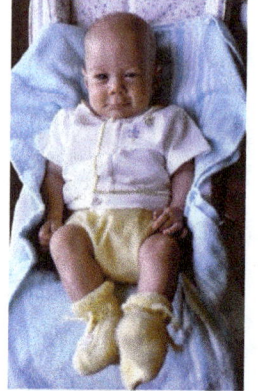

PHIL, JUNE 5

ARLENE, APS, GRAND CANYON

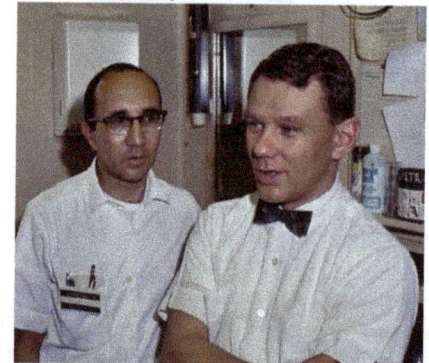

FRIEND, APS, GOING-IN-THE-U.S.-ARMY

APS, FORT SAM HOUSTON

HELEN, PHIL, MARK, HAROLD, AND KURT HEDEGARD, ARLENE, CALFORNIA

ARLENE, PHIL, MOM

1967-8, MOVE TO RENO, NEVADA

HAROLD, HELEN, PHIL, ARLENE, SAN FRAN.　　　PHIL, APRIL 28, 1967

PHIL, JUNE 5, 1968　　　LAURRIE, PHIL'S BD, DAVID, APRIL 28, 1968

KURT, MARK H, HAROLD, PHIL, HELEN, ASP　　　PHIL, JUNE 5, 1967

1969, ERIC ALLAN BORN MARCH 24,

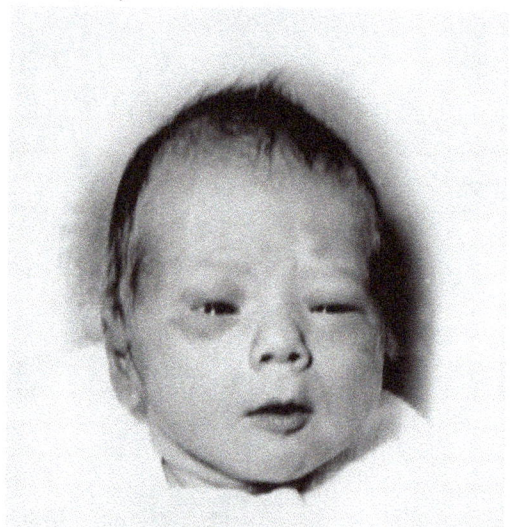

ERIC, MARCH 24   ERIC, APRIL 14

ARLENE, ERIC, PHIL, APRIL 1   PHIL, ERIC

PHIL, APS, APRIL 14   CHRIS, LAURRIE, CRAIG, MOM, ERIC, PHIL, SUZANNE, ROB, AND DAVID

1970, NEW HOME IN RENO, NEVADA

KURT, HAROLD AND MARK H

PHIL, 1640 MANZANITA LANE

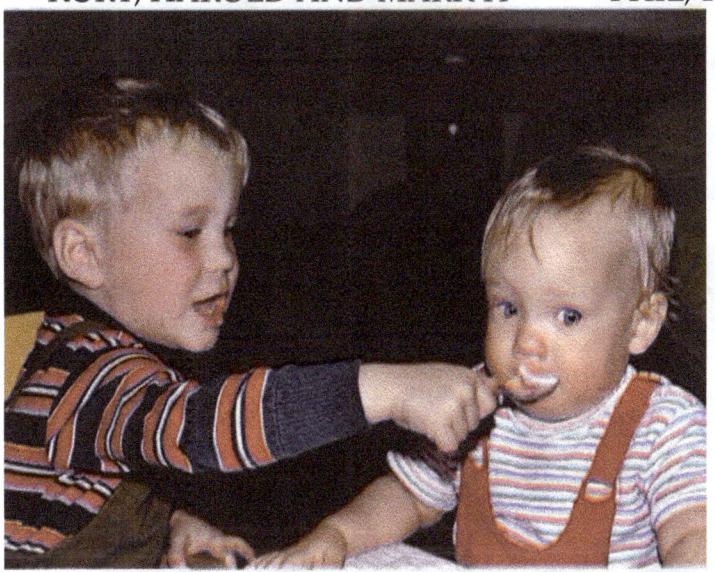
PHIL, ERIC, "FOOD FOR THOUGHT"

PHIL, ERIC, CHRISTMAS

ERIC, PHIL

ERIC, RENTED HOUSE ON LAKESIDE

1971, KRISTIN DIANE BORN MARCH 20

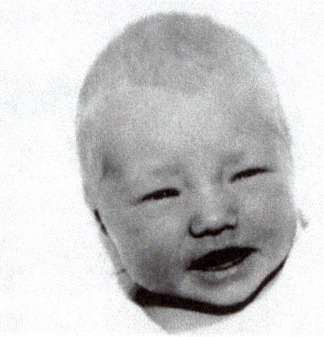 

KRISTIN, MARCH 20   KRISTIN, APRIL 28

LAURRIE, ERIC, DAVID, PHIL   PHIL, ERIC, PYRAMID LK

KRISTIN   ERIC

KRISTIN, HELEN, OCT. 1   KRISTIN, ERIC, APRIL 28

1972, TRIPS TO BODIE & VIRGIN ISLANDS

ERIC

APS, RON CUDEK, BOB CHURCH, MIDDLEFORK FLOAT TRIP

ERIC, PHIL, ARLENE & KRIS, BODIE, NV

ARLENE, VIRGIN ISLANDS

1973, TRIPS TO DENMARK & BUDAPEST

HAROLD, SVEN, FAMILY HOME   PHIL, ERIC, FREDERIKSBORG

PHIL, ERIC, LEGOLAND   PHIL, CHICAGO

PHIL, EINGER, ARLENE, ERIC   ARLENE, ERIC, PHIL, BUDAPEST GYPSY NIGHT

1974, OUR NEW TAHOE DONNER CABIN

PHIL, ERIC, ARLENE, KRIS, TDC   ERIC, PHIL, DAVID & LAURRIE WALKER, TDC

PHIL, KRIS, ERIC, DAVID, LAURRIE   PHIL, KRIS, ERIC

LAURRIE, KRIS, ERIC, PHIL, LOUISE, DAVID, ALCATRAZ   MOM, ERIC, ARLENE, PHIL, KRIS, CANADA TRAIN

—11—

1975, TRIPS TO UTAH AND ARIZONA

KRIS, ERIC, PHIL, EASTER

UNK, PHIL

PHIL, ERIC, KRIS, NAVAJO NATIONAL MOMUMENT

KRIS

BUTCH CASSIDY HOUSE, PHIL, ERIC, KRIS. UTAH

PHIL, ERIC, KRIS

1976, "BACK HOME AGAIN IN INDIANA"

KRIS, PHIL, ERIC, TAHOE DONNER

PHIL, TAHOE DONNER

ERIC

CRAIG, HARRIETT, ERIC, MIMI, KRIS, LOUISE, MOM,
SUZANNE, PHIL, ROB, DAVID, CHRIS, BOB, APS

KRIS, ERIC, PHIL, BROWN COUNTY, IND.

HAROLD, KRIS, PHIL, INDPLS

1977, LIFE IN RENO, NEVADA

DAVID, KRIS, PHIL, ERIC, OREGON　　　PHIL, 1640 MANZANITA

KRIS, DEATH VALLEY　　　KRIS, ERIC, 1ST DAY OF SCHOOL

ERIC, ARLENE, KRIS, HELEN, CHRISTMAS　　　PHIL, SNOW CAMPING

1978, TRIPS TO ALASKA & SAN FRANCISCO

ERIC, PHIL, KRIS, HALLOWEEN

ERIC

PHIL, ERIC, KRIS, DAVID WALKER
SAN FRANCISCO

ERIC, STUART STRINGHAM

KRIS, CHRISTMAS

DAVID, ERIC, KRIS, PHIL, MOM, ALASKA

1979, LIFE IN RENO, NEVADA

ROB, PHIL, CHRIS, ERIC, BLUE LAKE, NV

KRISTIN, TYLER HEDEGARD

PHIL, SCOTT & RON CUDEK, APS, CHUKAR HUNT

ERIC, DONNER LAKE

APS, ARLENE, ERIC, INDY 500 EXHIBIT

PHIL, KRIS, ERIC

1980, TRIPS TO PUERTO RICO & INDIANAPOLIS

CRAIG, KRIS, SUZANNE, BOWER'S MANSION
SIERRA NEVADA LAB PARTY

PHIL, WOOSTER HIGH

KRIS, DANIELLE H., INDIANAPOLIS
JUNE 5

KRIS, MIMI, BOB, ERIC, CHRIS,
PUERTO RICO

KRIS, JANE, ERIC, APS, ARLENE,
NAPA, CA

PHIL, KRIS, SUZANNE, CRAIG, BILL,
ERIC, APS, 1640 MANZANITA, RENO

1981, HUNTING AND FISHING

PHIL, ERIC, KRIS

ERIC, PHIL, CHUKAR HUNT

KRIS, PHIL, SALMON FISHING

ERIC BIRTHDAY

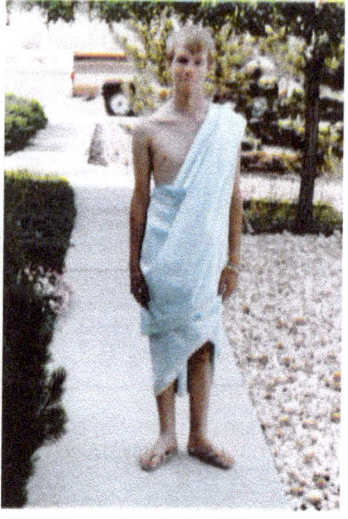

PHIL, WOOSTER HS

1982, NEW DONNER LAKE HOUSE

PHIL NEW PRINDLE SAILBOAT

REMODEL, DONNER LAKE HOUSE

ERIC, PHIL   ARLENE, PHIL, KRIS, ORIGINAL DL HOUSE

KRISTIN   ADOLF ROSENAUER, GORDON NITZ, DEER FEAST

1983, TRIP TO HAWAII

REX, MARK, AS, KURT & DICK

KRIS, HALLOWEEN

PATRICK KRETZ, PHIL, KRIS, ERIC, ARLENE, APS, HAWAII

HELEN, PHIL, ARLENE, KRIS

ERIC, HELEN, PHIL, KRIS

EARL, STU OLIVER, APS, ROY HOGAN, OWEN BOLSTAD, PHIL, DEER HUNT

1984, PHIL OFF TO MASSACHUSETTS INST. TECH.

APS, OFFICE AT UNRSOM

APS, PRESIDENT NSMA

PHIL OFF TO MASS. INST. TECH.

HELEN & PHIL AT MASS. INST. TECH.

KRISTIN

APS, ARLENE, PHIL AT NSMA MEETING

1985, CHICHÉN ITZA AND MEXICO

ERIC, CRAIG, SUZANNE, ROB, KRISTIN, CHRIS

RENO GALAXY CRASH

ERIC, MEXICO   PHIL, ERIC, CHICHEN ITZA, MEXICO

APS, MOM, BOB SOHN   ERIC, KRISTIN

1986, "GO IU" AND MINNESOTA CANOE TRIP

PHYLLIS CUDEK, APS, ARLENE, RON CUDEK, "GO IU"

ERIC, APS, HAWAII

KRIS, ERIC, HELEN, HAWAII TRIP

LORI, KURT, APS, AS, MINN. CANOE TRIP

BOB SOHN AND APS

1987, ERIC RENO HIGH GRADUATE

KRISTIN, MARK FERMOILE, JUNIOR ACHIEVEMENT FORMAL

ERIC SENIOR PROM

ARLENE, ERIC RENO HIGH GRAD, KRISTIN

KRISTIN, NEW VOLKSWAGEN

PHIL, EARL, DEER HUNT

1988, ERIC OFF TO UNIV. OF SO. CALIFORNIA

KRISTIN   ERIC

PHIL, ARLENE, ERIC, KRIS, CRUISE   ARLENE, APS, PHIL, ERIC, KRIS, CRUISE

APS, BOB COX, TOOLE, FLEENER, ROPP,   KRISTIN, CRUISE
MONTGOMERY, HARRY SMITH, HOWE REUNION

1989, PHIL MASSACHUSETTS INST. TECH. GRAD.

PHIL, LIZ   APS, PHIL MIT GRAD

KRIS, PHIL, SUZANNE, GREG   SUZANNE, GREG CARR

APS, KRIS & MARK F, SENIOR PROM   ARLENE, KRIS, APS

ARLENE, DICK, ALLAN, MARK H, REX, KURT   HARRIETT, ARLENE, APS, FL

—26—

1990, ERIC USC GRAD, LIZ/PHIL WEDDING, & KRIS TO UNIV. CALIFORNIA SANTA BARBARA

ARLENE, ERIC, APS, USC GRAD   LIZ, PHIL, MARRIED MAY 26

KRIS, TINA AMBLER, UCSB   MATTHEW, ERIC, ANDREW, MARK H, DONNER

PAT HAWN, LAURRIE, DAVID, PC   HELEN, ERIC, KRIS, APS, HAWAII

1991, KRISTIN SOHN, SEMESTER-AT-SEA

KRISTIN, SEMESTER-AT-SEA

MARY EDITH & BILL GANTZ,
ARLENE, IMELDA ROTH, DONNER LAKE

PHIL, ERIC, LIZ, ARLENE

MARK AND PAT HEDEGARD, APS

MARK FERMOILE, KRISTIN

1992, PISTOL CREEK AND BALTIMORE

KRISTIN, ARTILLERY LAKE, PC

KRISTIN, ARLENE, WILLIAMSBURG

ARLENE, KURT, KRISTIN, RENO

APS, PHIL, PISTOL CREEK

KRISTIN AND PUSS

APS, KRISTIN, BALTIMORE

1993, KRISTIN SOHN GRADUATE, UNIVERSITY CALIFORNIA SANTA BARBARA

APS, KRISTIN UCSB GRAD, ARLENE, ERIC

HELEN, MARY JANE, ARLENE

BILL, APS, FLORIDA

ERIC, PISTOL CREEK

ERIC, ARLENE, PHIL, LIZ, KRIS, SAN FRAN

APS, HARRIETT, BILL, CRAIG, FL

ERIC, KRIS, APS, CHANNEL ISLANDS

1994, ANTON PETER SOHN BORN NOVEMBER 29, WOODINVILLE, WASHINGTON

PETER, DECEMBR 9, APS

ERIC, APS, ARLENE, KRIS

ERIC MARCH 24

APS, KRIS, LIZ, PHIL, RUTH, ARLENE

LOUISE SOHN WALKER, APS

1995, ANTON PETER SOHN, ONE-YEAR-OLD

HELEN, KRISTIN   APS

MARK FERMOILE AND KRISTIN   PETER SOHN

ERIC   PETER, ARLENE

1996, ERIC ALLAN SOHN MD, UNIV. OF NEVADA RENO SCHOOL OF MEDICINE

ERIC ALLAN SOHN MD, UNRSOM

APS, KRIS, NEW ORLEANS   BILL, HARRIETT, ARLENE, PANNING FOR GOLD. CA

 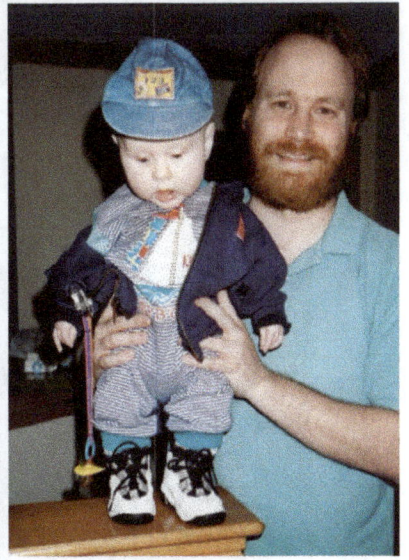

BILL. ARLENE, HARRIETT, CRAIG, YOLANDA, KRIS, FL   PETER, PHIL

1997, KERRY THOMAS SOHN BORN MARCH 10, ALEXANDER WISE SOHN BORN JUNE 24

KRISTIN, KERRY ERIC, KERRY

CRAIG, KRISTIN, YOLANDA, JUNE 14 APS, KERRY, ARLENE

KERRY, ARLENE, ERIC, HELEN PETER, ALEX

1998, REX, DICK, ARLENE (SOHN), ALAN, HELEN, MARK AND KURT HEDEGARD

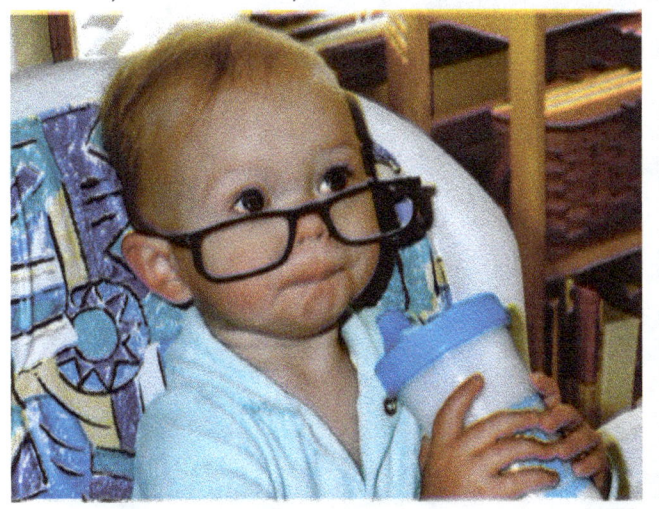

KERRY SOHN   PETER, PHIL, ALEX, LIZ

PETER, KRISTIN   KERRY

REX, DICK, ARLENE, ALAN, HELEN, MARK, KURT   KERRY

1999, BRADY CARSON SOHN BORN JUNE 9

ERIC, KERRY, APS, BRADY

BRADY, KERRY, DEC. 14

APS, KERRY, PETER, ALEX, DONNER LK

KRISTIN APS, ARLENE, EPHESUS

ERIC, PHIL, ARLENE, APS, KRIS, DL

APS, BRADY, KERRY, RENO

2000, SIERRA MORGAN SOHN BORN SEPTEMBER 27

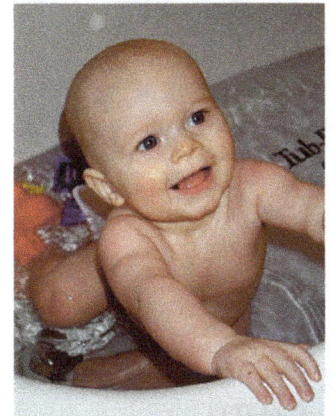

BRADY SOHN   KERRY SOHN

KERRY, PETER   APS, ARLENE, BILL, HARRIETT, FL

PETER, LEGOLAND   RUTH, PETER, PHIL, ALEX, ARLENE

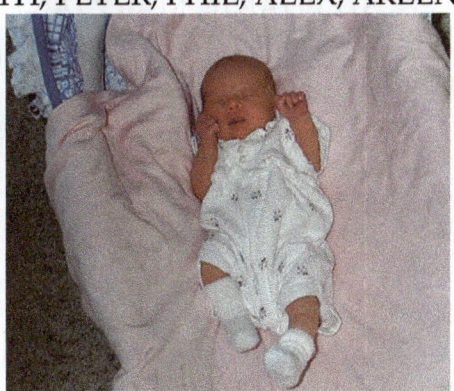

ARLENE, BOB, MIMI, KRIS, FL   SIERRA

2001, TRIPS TO TAHITI AND IRELAND

KRIS, APS, ARLENE, TAHITI

ALEX, KERRY, PETER   ALEX, PETER

KURT, HELEN, STEPHANIE, MARY JANE   BRADY, KERRY, CUPERTINO

ARLENE, HARRIETT, BILL, IRELAND   SIERRA

2002, PISTOL CREEK AND WOODINVILLE

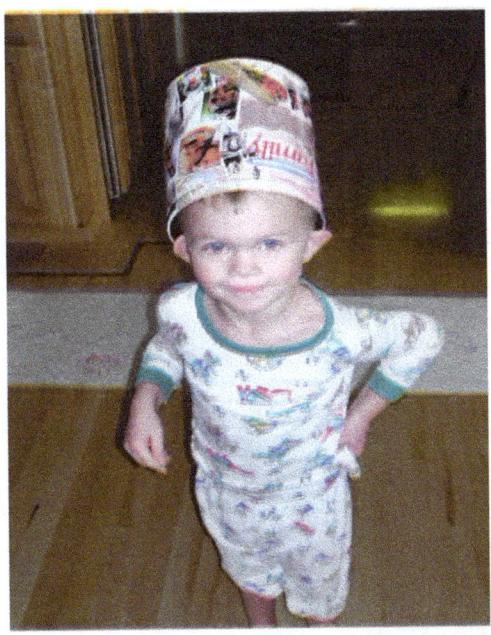

BRADY

SIERRA, NEW LEXUS

LIZ, PETER, PHIL, WOODINVILLE

KRIS, ARLENE, SAN DIEGO

HARRIETT, BILL, ARLENE, APS, PISTOL CREEK

2003, KRISTIN/MARK'S WEDDING, AUGUST 9

MARK FERMOILE AND KRISTIN

KRISTIN, ARLENE

APS, KRISTIN

SUZANNE OSTER, KRIS, JAY JAY LOWDEN

KERRY, BRADY, ERIC, KRISTI SOHN,
MARK F, KRIS, SIERRA, APS, ARLENE

2004, BRADY SOHN'S FIRST FISH

SIERRA, SPOKANE   ARLENE, SIERRA

HARRIETT, APS, ARLENE, CA   ROB, ARLENE, MIMI, APS, PC

KERRY, ERIC, SIERRA   PHIL, KRIS, APS, ARLENE, ERIC, PC

KERRY, PC   BRADY, KERRY, PC

2005, PISTOL CREEK AND TRIP TO EGYPT

ERIC, KERRY, MARK, BRADY, KRIS, APS, ALEX, AS, PETER, PHIL, PC

SIERRA   APS, ARLENE, EGYPT

BILL, BOB, LOUISE   BRADY, MAURIZA, KERRY, SIERRA

APS, BILL, BOB, FL   BRADY, ERIC, KERRY'S BD, AS, APS, SIERRA

2006, TRIP TO AUSTRALIA

KERRY, SIERRA, BRADY, TO-SCHOOL

APS, ARLENE, BOB, MIMI, CA

ALEX, BRADY, PETER, KERRY, SIERRA, PC

APS, AS, AUSTRALIA

APS, ALEX, SIERRA, KERRY, BRADY, PHIL

BRADY, SIERRA, KERRY

SIERRA, FRIENDS, HALLOWEEN

HARRIETT, BILL, AS, APS, NAPA

2007, TRIPS TO SCOTLAND AND FLORIDA

PHIL, KRISTIN, ERIC, PISTOL CREEK

BILL, HARRIETT, APS, AS, BODIE, NV

BRADY, ALEX, SIERRA, PETER, KERRY

GLENDA & GENE TOOLE, AS, SCOTLAND

APS, ARLENE, HARIETT, BILL, FL

—44—

2008, TRIP TO ALASKA

MARK, KRIS, AS, APS, CHRISTMAS

ARLENE, MARK H., BILL, FL

BRADY, ALEX, SIERRA, PETER, KERRY, ALASKA

ERIC, BRADY, ARLENE, APS, LK TAHOE

APS, GENE, GLENDA, AS, HOUSTON

GLENDA, APS, ARLENE, HOUSTON

2009, MAURIZA/ERIC WEDDING & APS' RETIREMENT

SIERRA ARLENE, PACIFICA WRECK, OR

MAURIZA, ERIC, HAWAII PHYLLIS, APS' RETIRE, AS, RON

APS, BRADY, KRIS, KERRY, ERIC, SIERRA BRADY, RENO
PHIL, PETER, ALEX, ARLENE, PC

SIERRA, KRIS, DONNER LK BILL, LOUISE, BOB, APS, FL

2010, KRISTIN'S AWARD AT UNIVERSITY OF NEVADA RENO SCHOOL OF MED.

ARLENE, APS, HAWAII, USC GAME   KERRY, SPOKANE

BRADY, DONNER LK   LIZ, ALEX, PHIL, PETER, WOODINVILLE

KRIS' AWARD, ARLENE, APS, UNRSOM   BRADY, ERIC SPOKANE

ALEX, MAURIZA, PETER, APS, ERIC, SIERRA,   BOB, PISTOL CREEK
KRIS, ARLENE, PHIL, BRADY, KERRY, PC

2011, ISABELLA JOLIE SOHN BORN FEBUARY 27

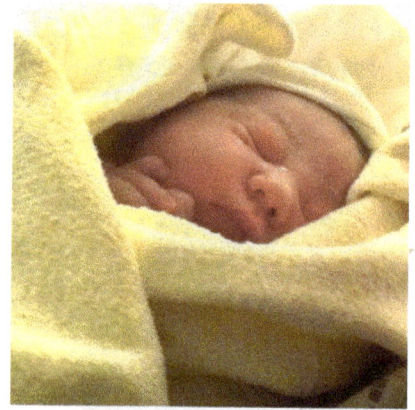
ISABELLA, FEB. 27

BRADY, ERIC, SIERRA, ISABELLA

SIERRA, KRISTIN, ISABELLA

APS, ARLENE BD, 4/23

MIMI, CHRIS, BOB

APS, LOUISE, BOB, BILL, FA

ALEX, PETER, PHIL

KERRY, AS, SIERRA, APS, ISABELLA, BRADY

2012, KRISTIN SOHN MD, UNIVERSITY OF NEVADA RENO SCHOOL OF MED.

COLE, BRADY, SIERRA, ERIC, KERRY, PC

PETER

ARLENE, APS, HARRIETT, BILL, CA

BRADY, KERRY, 4 FRIENDS, USC

KERRY, AS, SIERRA, APS, ERIC, BRADY, COLE, PC

ISABELLA, MAURIZA

KRIS, APS, ERIC, ARLENE

KERRY, BRADY, ISABELLA, MAURIZA, ERIC, SIERRA

2013, ARLENE/ANTON 50TH WEDDING ANNIVERSITY

ISABELLA, DL   KERRY, ISABELLA, BRADY, SIERRA, DL

SIERRA, ISABELLA, MAURIZA, DISNEY CRUISE   APS, PETER, AS, PHIL, ALEX, PC

ARLENE/APS 50TH WEDDING ANNIVERSITY   PETER, EAGLE SCOUT

2014, PETER GRADUATE, WOODINVILLE HIGH SCHOOL

PETER HS GRAD, WOODINVILLE

BOB, APS, BILL, FLORIDA

MARK F, KRISTIN, ARLENE, APS, DONNER

SIERRA, PISTOL CREEK

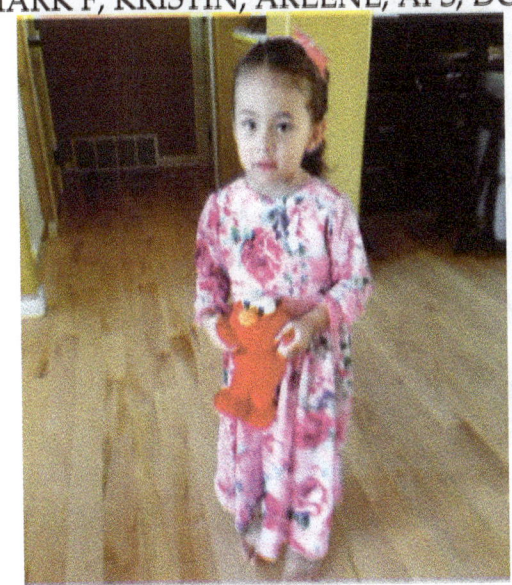
ISABELLA

PHIL, ARLENE, ERIC, APS, PISTOL CREEK

2015, KERRY GRADUATE, SPOKANE HIGH SCHOOL

ALAN, REX, DICK, AS, MARK, KURT, INDPLS

ISABELLA   ARLENE, KRIS RESIDENCY GRAD, APS

ISABELLA, PISTOL CREEK   ERIC, BRADY, SPOKANE

KERRY HS GRAD, SPOKANE   PHIL, KRIS, APS, ARLENE, ERIC, DONNER

2016, ALEX GRADUATE, WOODINVILLE HIGH SCHOOL

ALEX, MAURIZA, ERIC, Kris, AS, ISABELLA, APS, BRADY, KERRY, Phil, PC

LIZ, ALEX HS GRAD, PETER, AS, PHIL

ISABELLA, KERRY, PC

BILL, HARRIETT, AS, APS, DL

APS, KERRY, ERIC, PC

KRIS, MARK, RENO

HARRIETT, BILL, SUZANNE, GREG, AS, APS

2017, VISIT WITH BILL AND HARRIETT IN FLORIDA

ARLENE, HARIETT, BILL

CRAIG, BILL, FLORIDA

KERRY, ARLENE, DONNER LAKE

SIERRA, KRISTIN, PISTOL CREEK

ISABELLA, APS, DONNER LAKE

APS, KRIS, ARLENE, SACRAMENTO

2018, CHRISTMAS WITH KRIS/MARK IN RENO

KERRY, ERIC, BRADY, APS, MATT SCHMITT, PISTOL CREEK

APS, KRIS, ARLENE

MARK F, KRIS, ARLENE, APS, CHRISTMAS

PETER, APS, ALEX, RENO

APS, ISABELLA, KRIS, ERIC, DONNER LK

2019, KERRY JOINS NAVY, PETER UA GRADUATE

KRIS, ARLENE, APS' 84ᵀᴴ BD   ISABELLA, RENO

ERIC, KERRY NAVY   KENNEDY, SIERRA ALABAMA U.

PETER, UNIVERSITY OF ARIZONA GRADUATE

ISABELLA BACK TO SCHOOL   ISABELLA, SIERRA   KRIS, KEY WEST

2020, KRISTIN GETS A BMW
AND SIERRA IN NEW ORLEANS

ISABELLA, KERRY, ERIC, SIERRA, BRADY, SPOKANE

ALEX, LIZ, Phil, PETER, UTAH

KRISTIN, NEW BMW

SIERRA, NEW ORLEANS

2021, BRADY ASU GRAD, AS/APS 58ᵀᴴ WEDD. ANNIV.

ERIC, BRADY ASU GRADUATE   KERRY, CAMP LEJEUNE

ERIC, MAURIZA   ISABELLA

ARLENE/APS, 58ᵀᴴ ANNIV.   ERIC, KERRY. CAMP LEJEUNE

2022, LIZ AND PHIL AT THE KENTUCKY DERBY

Phil, LIZ, KENTUCKY DERBY

ERIC, KERRY, CAMP LEJEUNE

KERRY, FRIENDS, CAMP LEJEUNE

YOLANDA, GRACE, FRIEND, CRAIG

ERIC, ISABELLA, APS, DONNER

ERIC, SIERRA, ALA U

KRIS, MARK, PROSPECTORS CLUB

—59—

2023, SIERRA, UNIV. OF ALABAMA GRADUATE

SIERRA, AU Graduation

BOB SOHN, APS, RENO

BRADY, SIERRA, AU GRADUATION

BRADY, KRISTIN, ERIC, RENO

KRIS, MARK F, NEW ORLEANS

2023, ARLENE/ANTON 60TH WEDDING ANNIV.

ISABELLA, PETER, BRADY, APS, ARLENE, KERRY, SIERRA, ALEX

MARK, KRIS, ISABELLA, SIERRA, ERIC, KERRY, AS, BRADY, APS, PETER, PHIL, LIZ, ALEX

BRADY, ISABELLA, ERIC, SIERRA, KERRY, APS, AS, PHIL, LIZ, PETER, ALEX, KRIS, MARK

POSTSCRIPT: SKY'S-THE-LIMIT
"WAY UP IN MY FLYING MACHINE"

APS: At Fort Ord in 1966, I joined the pilot school and took instructions in a Cessna 150 from August 8, 1966 until October 27 for a total of 13 hours and 18 minutes. From October 27, 1966, until April 21, 1969, I made 16 solo flights for a total of 24 hours and 49 minutes. I discontinued pursuing a pilot's license when I was sent to Vietnam. (Information from *"Pilot Flight Record and Log Book"*)

Bill: I bought and picked up Cessna Skyhawk at the Cessna factory in 1974. I owned it for over 10 years and flew over 300 hours. I flew to Miami to attend Instrument Flight School and kept it in a T-Hanger at Metro Airport on east 96th street.

INDEX

A
Alexander, Mary Jane	30, 38
Ambler, Tina	27

B
Bolstad. Owen	20

C
Carr, Greg	26, 53
Carr, Suzanne Sohn	6, 13, 17, 22, 26, 53
Church, Bob	9
Cox, Bob	25
Cudek, Phyllis	23, 46
Cudek, Ronald	9, 16, 23, 46
Cudek, Scott	16

F
Fermoile, Kristin Sohn	8, 11, 12, 14, 15, 16, 17, 18, 19, 20, 21, 22, 23, 24, 25, 26, 27, 28, 29, 30, 31, 32, 33, 34, 35, 36, 38, 39, 40, 41, 44, 45, 46, 47, 48, 50, 51, 52, 53, 54, 55, 56, 57, 58, 59, 60, 61
Fermoile, Mark	24, 26, 27, 28, 32, 40, 45, 50, 51, 53, 55, 59, 60, 61
Fleener, Jim	25

G
Gleason, Ruth	31, 37
Granz, Bill	28
Granz, Mary Edith	28

H
Hawn, Pat	27
Hedegard, Alan	35
Hedegard, Andrew	27
Hedegard, Danielle	17
Hedegard, Dick	20, 26, 35, 52
Hedegard, Harold	4, 5, 7, 10, 13
Hedegard, Helen	4, 5, 8, 14, 20, 21, 23, 27, 30, 34, 35, 38
Hedegard, Jane	17
Hedegard, Kurt	4, 5, 7, 20, 23, 26, 29, 35, 38, 52
Hedegard, Mark	4, 5, 7, 20, 26, 27, 28, 35, 45, 52
Hedegard, Mathew	27
Hedegard, Pat	28
Hedegard, Rex	20, 10, 35, 52
Hedegard, Stephanie	38
Hedegard, Tyler	16
Hogan, Roy	20
Held, Jay Jay	40

K
Kretz, Patrick	20

M
Montgomery, Bob	25

N
Nitz, Gordon	19

O
Oliver, Stuart	20
Oster, Suzanne	40

R
Ropp, Bill	25
Rosenauer, Adolf	19
Roth,, Imelda	28

S
Schmitt, Matt	55
Smith, Harry	25
Sohn, Alex	34, 36, 37, 38, 42, 43, 45, 46, 47, 49, 50, 53, 55, 57, 61
Sohn, Anton Paul	1, 2, 3, 4, 6, 9, 13, 16, 17, 20, 21, 22, 23, 25, 26, 27, 28, 29, 31, 32, 33, 34, 41, 42, 44, 45, 46, 47, 48, 49, 50, 52, 53, 54, 55, 56, 58, 59, 60, 61, 62
Sohn. Anton Peter	31, 33, 34, 35, 36, 37, 38, 39, 40, 42, 43, 44, 45, 46, 47, 48, 49, 50, 51, 53, 55, 56, 57, 61
Sohn, Anton Phillip	4, 5, 6, 7, 8, 9, 10, 11, 12, 13, 14, 15, 16, 17, 18, 19, 20, 21, 22, 24, 25, 26, 27, 28, 29, 30, 33, 35, 36, 37, 39, 41, 42, 43, 44, 46, 47, 48, 50, 51, 52, 53, 57, 59, 61
Sohn, Arlene	1, 2, 3, 4, 6, 9, 10, 11, 13, 14, 16, 19, 20, 21, 23, 24, 25, 26, 27, 28, 29, 30, 31, 32, 33, 34, 36, 37, 38, 39, 40, 41, 42, 43, 44, 45, 46, 47, 48, 49, 50, 51, 52, 53, 54, 55, 56, 58, 61

Sohn, Brady	36, 37, 38, 39, 40, 41, 42, 43, 44, 45, 46, 47, 48, 49, 50, 52, 53, 55, 57, 60, 61	Sohn. Yolanda	33, 34, 59
Sohn, Bill	17, 30, 31, 33, 37, 36, 39, 42, 43, 44,45, 46, 48, 49, 51, 53, 54, 62	Sorensen, Einger	10
		Stringum, Stuart	15

T

Toole, Gene	25, 44, 45
Toole, Glenda	44, 45

W

Walker, David	5, 6, 8, 11, 13, 14, 15, 27
Walker, Laurrie	5, 6, 8, 11, 27
Walker, Louise Sohn	11, 13, 31, 42, 46, 48

Sohn, Bob	13, 17, 22, 23, 37, 41, 42, 43, 46, 47, 48, 51, 53, 60
Sohn, Christopher	6, 13, 16, 17, 22, 48
Sohn, Craig	6, 17, 22, 33, 34, 54, 59
Sohn, Elizabeth	26, 27, 28, 31, 35, 39, 50, 57, 59
Sohn, Eric	6, 7, 8, 9, 10, 11, 12, 13, 14, 15, 16, 17, 18, 19, 20, 22, 23, 24, 25, 27, 28, 30, 31, 32, 33, 34, 36, 40, 41, 42, 44, 45, 46, 47, 48, 49, 50, 51, 52, 53, 55, 56, 58, 59, 60, 61
Sohn, Grace	59
Sohn, Harriett	13, 26, 33, 37, 38, 39, 41, 43, 44, 49, 53, 54
Sohn, Isabella	48, 49, 50, 51, 52, 53, 54, 55, 57, 58, 59, 61
Sohn, Kerry	34, 35, 36, 37, 38, 40, 41, 42, 43, 43, 44, 45, 46, 47, 48, 49, 50, 52, 53, 54, 56, 57, 58, 59, 61
Sohn, Kristie	40
Sohn, Mauriza	42, 46, 47, 49, 50, 53, 58
Sohn, Mimi	13, 17, 37, 41, 43, 48
Sohn, Rob Anthony	6, 13, 16, 22
Sohn, Ruth Marie	2, 4, 6, 11, 13, 15, 22
Sohn, Sierra	37, 38, 39, 40, 41, 42, 43, 44, 45, 46, 47, 48, 49, 50, 52, 53, 54, 56, 57, 59, 60, 61

www.ingramcontent.com/pod-product-compliance
Lightning Source LLC
Chambersburg PA
CBHW080627170426
43209CB00007B/1534